# Quest

## The Journey
## IS
## the Treasure

## John Chuchman

# Discoveries

Moments ............................... 4
Life .................................... 6
Freedom ............................... 7
Within ................................ 9
Proof ................................. 11

Setbacks ............................. 13
Attention ............................ 15
Now .................................. 17
Darkness and Light .............. 20
Compassion ....................... 24

Love ................................. 27
Awareness .......................... 30
Present Moment ................. 34
Listening ........................... 36
Silence .............................. 38

Simplicity .......................... 40
Judgment ........................... 42
Faith ................................. 46
Mystery ............................. 51
Balance ............................. 56

Wisdom .............................. 59
Creation ............................. 62
Letting Go .......................... 65

This Book

is intended as an encouragement

to all those who have traveled

life's journey

without having embarked on

the Quest.

The author hopes

it demonstrates that

it is never too late

and

that the Quest

is laden with Treasure

beyond measure.

## Moments

Thank You, God,

for those Moments of Opening
which touch me
in seemingly random,
unpredictable fashion
at times transforming me.

They come
when the chatter of my mind stills
and my concerns about accomplishing
fall away.

When I can be Silent,
You bring
Deep Serenity and Harmony.

Thank You
for the Moments of Opening
when I am Listening
to a friend in grief
as my judgments and assumptions
fall away
and my heart opens.

I seem to be totally present
when the barriers
between others and me
melt away
and the radiance of Compassion
emerges.

Thank You for the Moments of Opening
when I'm alone
and my need for busyness and
satisfaction and clamoring thoughts
cease.

In Silence,
I find aloneness
without loneliness or alienation,
aloneness that speaks of a rich
Completeness and Oneness
with the Maker of the Universe.

Moments of Silence
remind me of
what really matters in life.
They remind me
how important it is
to live fully as
an Aware Compassionate human being.

## <u>Life</u>

My past accomplishments, credentials, possessions
gave no true sense
of quality and value
to my life.

My ideas or memories
did not liberate, nor heal.
My life is given some quality
as I begin to learn
to truly Love
and to leave the results
to God.

No one can tell me
exactly how to live my life,
no matter how wise or loving
that person.
No one has ever lived my life before.

I, myself, am learning
to live with Integrity
and Wisdom
and Love.
I seek to live what is True,
to live what is here,
Right Now.

## Freedom

I long for a connection to God
through all things,
which I know is present
in any moment,
that my heart can open to it.

I knew
there are hundreds of ways
to travel my spiritual path
and thousands of spiritual paths
that I can travel.
But, each one of them
begins with the next step I take,
the next words I speak,
the next songs I sing,
the way I touch an other or
the way an other touches me.

My Freedom in this life
comes not from
things I possess
(possessions seem to enslave)
but from my ability
to be Open to each Moment,
to God within me.

My Freedom
is simply Letting Go and
being fully Open and Honest and Loving
toward the next moment,
the next person,
the fullness of life
as it is.

## Within

I long to find God
within me,
the Source of Great Compassion,
Trust, and Wholeness.
I believe
that God within me
inspires me
to Comfort and Support
a friend in need
and
intervenes
to prevent the infliction of pain
on an other.

Perhaps by living this way,
I can show the way and
teach and serve
by how empty I am,
how deeply I Listen,
how Loving my heart has become.

I think God in me
grieves at the pain in the world
and rejoices in
the Happiness and Love that I find.

When I am vitally connected
to God in my own heart,
I appreciate and share
with all humanity.
I taste true Wholeness and Trust
in my Awareness of
the connectedness of all things
with each other and
with God.

## Proof

My Compassion and Love
do not need grand gestures or
dramatic expression.
My opportunities
to Love, Forgive, Reverence
are many.
Each time I respond to
the needs of an other,
I act as a conscious helper
in the creation of a world
at Peace.

Each of my responses,
no matter how ordinary,
is Worthy, Significant, and
makes a difference.

The greatness of my Heart
lies in my not demanding proof
that my responses of Love and Care
make a difference.

The vastness of my Love
lies in not needing evidence of
the impact of my Caring.

My Faith in Love
sustains me.
The richness of my Caring
nurtures me.
In not asking for confirmation,
approval or reward,
I am Free
to live simply
in the Spirit of Reverence of Love.

## Setbacks

**This Quest
requires Courage and Strength.
I often call upon deep inner resources,
for I am in unfamiliar territory
and
fear and doubt and uncertainty
are my constant companions.**

**There have been many detours
and diversions,
typical of all journeys.
Again and again,
I have had to make new beginnings,
and move in new directions.**

**There have been no signposts saying,
"Right on, John!"
At times,
I felt like I lost my way
as I have fallen, floundered,
made mistakes,
and doubted myself.**

I am learning
to accept difficulty with Graciousness
and to grow through my mistakes.
Somehow, the Spirit leads me
to a place of Serenity and Truth
amid the storms and difficulties.
I am learning in this Quest
that Awareness and Trust
are fundamental.
I try to nurture these qualities
in order to transcend my concepts of
winning, losing, accomplishing, and
achieving.

## Attention

I am discovering that
a life of Awareness and Sensitivity
depends on me
Paying Attention.

My Growth
is marked not by grand gestures
or visible acclamations,
but by my extending Loving Attention
to the minutest particulars
on my Quest.

Every one of my Relationships,
every thought,
every gesture
becomes Blessed by God with meaning
through the wholehearted attention
I bring to it.

In the complexity of my mind
and my life,
I often forgot the power of Attention.
Yet, without it,
I live only on the surface of existence.

Only simple Attention
allows me to
truly Listen to the song of a bird,
deeply see the glory of an autumn leaf,
touch the heart of an other,
be touched by an other's heart.

# Now

I have come to realize that
in order to Love Wholeheartedly,
I need to be fully present in the Now.
I am learning that
in order to learn from this moment,
I must be fully awake in it.

I used to think
my life was an endless stretch of time
extending beyond the horizon.
I savored memories of my past and
fantasies of my future
often losing myself
in preoccupation with them.
In doing so,
I postponed the opening of my heart,
deferring my Quest for connectedness.

I discovered
the unpredictability of my life,
the uncertainty of my days,
gaining a sense of
Urgency and Passion
about my relationship
to the Present Moment
and to God.

I discovered
that I can only live in Love and Wisdom
Here
and that I can only Open up my Heart
Now,
that God is Here and Now.

I am learning that
Attention is Sensitivity
is Connectedness.

Attention
reveals to me
the joys and sorrows around me.
The Spirit within
helps me not to retreat from pain,
but to ask
how I can participate in Healing.

I have experienced
the greatest healing
in the smallest gestures,
a Loving Touch,
A Caring Word,
a Compassionate Heart.

Attention connects me
with my own thoughts, feelings,
yearnings.

I am learning
to Listen inwardly
without judgment or resistance
and in the process
begin to learn and understand myself.

Attention is a Source of Wisdom.

But it can begin
only in this moment
in which I now find myself.

## Darkness and Light

I had looked for
my achievements, my success,
my possessions
to bring light into my life,
into my heart.
I looked to the future,
for the attainment of accomplishments,
in my Quest for Wholeness,
as if it were somewhere else.

When I focused on my self-interests,
I ended up feeling
unsatisfied, misdirected, shallow.
The insecurity that followed
led to blame, control, self-protection
and even hostility.

I often tried to anesthetize myself
which only served to
increase my isolation,
my separateness.
In these dark times,
I found myself longing
for some ideal future or
some magic formula
to make me whole.

In learning the Art of Living Fully,
I began to see Light amid my darkness,
began to help others Heal
and thus, Heal myself.

I am learning
that Living in Peace
requires Great Love,
that Peace
is not rest,
but Love in Action.

I had to be willing
not to turn away from
life's shadows,
not to shun the darkness,
but to turn toward them.

In moving into the darkness,
I began to cast away
fears, self-doubt, despair.
I found that
darkness is not my opponent,
but that,
my denial or rejection of it
is.

In life's difficulties,
I discovered a sense of what is
Everlasting Unquenchable Light.
St. John of the Cross offered,
"If a person wishes to be sure
of the road upon which they tread,
they must close their eyes
and walk in the dark."

There I found
True Compassion
and
Greatness of Spirit.

As I turned to the shadows
in my own life
with an Open Heart,
I stopped reacting and resisting.
I began to Understand
and to Heal.
I simply needed to feel deeply.

It needed to be done
not so much with open eyes
as with my inner senses,
my heart, my intuition.
I began Seeing
and Listening closely
to the Mystery right in front of me.

Listening and Feeling and Opening
set me free.
When I resisted and
sought light somewhere else,
I remained separate from
what is,
separate from God.

Learning to Listen inwardly,
I discovered
new depths of Calmness,
new resources of Energy,
new Effectiveness.

Those shadows
I had previously counted
as adversaries
became my most profound
teachers.
I have tried to meet them with
Grace, Serenity, and Forgiveness.

In doing so, I have learned that
Peace is not the opposite of hardship
nor Light the result of darkness ending.
Peace resulted with my own capacity
to be with suffering
without judgment, prejudice, or
resistance.

## Compassion

I discovered an energy in me
to heal and be healed
through an Openheartedness
to each moment.

I found out
that to live in a Sacred way,
I need to connect
to other human beings
and to acknowledge
our interdependence
and Love.

I am learning that
Compassion is that singular quality
of Heart
that has the power to transform
resentment into Forgiveness,
hatred into Friendship,
anger into Loving Kindness.

I found a most precious quality
of my being
which allows me to extend
Warmth, Sensitivity, Openness
to those around me
and myself.

I learned that Compassion
is so much more than pity.
It is a deep heartfelt Caring
for the Dignity, Well-being,
and Integrity
of every life form,
from the smallest
to the most powerful.

I don't think
anyone is exempt from the need for
Compassion,
for no one is exempt from pain.
*We are healed by*
*the Loving Presence*
*of each other.*

I found that
the greatest of human arts,
Kindness,
is really very simple,
yet with it
came great Dignity and
tremendous Integrity
for others
and for me.

There seems to be
no barrier or obstacle
that Loving Kindness
cannot overcome.
I believe
it can change the world.

Life continues to present me
with countless moments
that call me to
Greater and Greater
Depths of Compassion.
I had often lost
the connection to compassion
in busyness, ambition, and pride.
But then,
I seemed to find it again and
reconnect with my Creator.

A simple touching of those around me
with Kindness
reconnects me to God.
In those moments of Compassion,
remarkable things happened.

## Love

I know how it feels
to live in
anger, fear, guilt, alienation.
I know too
what it feels like
to be filled to overflowing
with Love.

I found that Compassion
is not some future goal,
Nor is it the result of
my own spiritual effort.
Strangely enough,
opportunities for Love and Compassion
lie in those moments
when I am tempted to react
with prejudice, rejection,
disdain, or anger.
In those moments,
I asked myself
if I really wanted
to travel a path of alienation
or if were possible to find
within myself
the Forgiveness and Care
that allowed me
to touch the heart of an other.

When I felt lost,
there were always beacons of light.
They were rarely cast
by powerful or holy people
or people with great answers
to the worlds dilemmas.
Most often,
they seemed to radiate from
simple ordinary people,
who in their encounters with life,
have been transformed
and have learned
how to respond to the world
with the Simplicity and Power
of Faith, Love, and Compassion.

I now know
there is no greater power
than Love.

I was asked again and again
to summon from within me
the Spirit of Compassion
and Openheartedness.
Perhaps, this is why I am here,
to learn this lesson.
I could not fall back on
my credentials, accomplishments,
or possessions.

I had to fall back on
my Humanity,
my God.

My ordinariness
underlies all my experiences,
all I do.
Like all others,
I was born and will die.

But I will not die
never having Loved.

## Awareness

Within myself,
I have discovered an extraordinary gift,
my capacity to be Aware.
This Blessing
allows me to make choices
and to sense possibilities open to me.
It empowers me
to Learn and to Grow.
It means that I need not be driven
by protectiveness and hostility,
but that I can nurture my capacity for
Understanding and Forgiveness.

I have not yet plumbed the depths
of my Awareness.
How close can I truly come
to an other?
How deeply can I feel the wind
that only seems to brush me?
How attuned can I be to
the changing rhythms of the universe?
How Free can I be?

The only thing I know for sure
about Awareness is that
it removes all distance,
it shatters superficiality,
it connects me
with my Master's Heart,
it allows me to meet life's challenges
with Greatness of Heart.


Finding my way to authentic
Awakening
presented me with
an immense challenge.
I wanted to listen to
the voices of those around me
which seemed to hold answers
to life's questions.
The world abounds with
advice, solutions, formulas
and I have been truly inspired
by teachers and sages
past and present.

But I now know
no single earthly source
holds the Truth hot-line.
There is no one right path.

It seems that
the Truly Wise
have listened to the Wisdom
in their own Hearts
and traveled their own paths.

No one can travel my path for me,
nor tell me how to do so.
In trusting that
Wisdom, Joy, Awakening
are my spiritual heritage,
I needed to discover
what it is
that awakened them in me.

No one can free me
from my confusion, attachments,
shadows
except me,
with God's help.

I know that the aloneness of
my Quest
is not an aloneness of
alienation or withdrawal.
I am supported
by the generations gone before
who applaud and inspire
my Quest.

*My Quest connects me*
*with millions of Companions.*

I felt doubt and inadequacy.
I wondered how to cross the bridge
from confusion to clarity.
Through it all
I have been Blessed
with the most precious gift,
Awareness.

Through Awareness
comes my Transformation.
Through Awareness
I am able to penetrate
the veils of confusion
that limited me.
Through Awareness
I can connect with and use
my inner resources of
Energy, Focus, Love.

I am learning that
being Aware means
being wholeheartedly present
in each moment,
present with myself and
with whatever or whomever
it brings me.

## Present Moment

When I connect with
the present moment,
I can set aside anxiety over the future
and what I might gain, lose, or become
When I connect with
the present moment,
I can set aside preoccupations
with the past and
burdens of guilt, regret, resentment.

My Awareness
illuminates what is actually here
one moment at a time.
It is in the present moment
that I am able to be
Open to God,
and to Learn.

I am learning
that the Present Moment is
the most profound and challenging
teacher
I will ever meet.
It is a Compassionate teacher,
extending no judgment,
no censure,
no measurement of success or failure.

The Present Moment
is a mirror
in whose reflection
I learn to see myself
and God
in me.

When I can look in the mirror
without deluding myself,
I can find Wisdom.
In the Present Moment,
I can see
what contributes to
confusion and discord
and what contributes to
Harmony and Understanding.

In the Present Moment
I can see the relationship between
pain and its cause
and
Love and its Source.
In it,
I can see
what connects me and
what alienates me.

## Listening

Listening inwardly,
I am learning
that I do not need experts
to define my way.
Listening inwardly,
I am learning
I need clear and direct
Inner Attunement
to God within me.
In Listening,
I can understand what it is
I need to let go
and what I need to develop.

My Quest
differs only in superficial form
and details
from yours.
There is no living being
that does not share
our Yearning for God.

To Live Fully,
To Love Well,
I now know that I must learn
to experience fully
the Present Moment.

I now know
that the heart of my spiritual life
is to fully live
in the ever changing reality of
the Present Moment.

## Silence

What I seek
is not found in more sights and sounds
or tastes or thoughts
but in the living reality
of each moment I touch
with Love and Understanding.

The clutter in my life
blinded me
to the precious Spirituality
that surrounds and is within me.
I had often become
possessed and imprisoned
by the chains of
my accomplishments and
accumulations.

The noise
created by my own busyness
deafened me
to the Wonder of Silence.

I had equated Silence with
absence and privation.

My lack of silence
only served to make me
poorer in spirit.

I know
that I do not need to retreat
to a monastery
to discover the world of silence.
I do not need to withdraw
from the world
to discover Simplicity of Heart.

It is not a matter
of how much I have or don't have;
It's a matter
of how much I try to hold on to.

## <u>Simplicity</u>

Simplicity
is an act of Compassion
for myself
and for those around me.

I discovered
that when I let go
of planning for the future,
when I let go
of reliving the past,
when I let go
of protecting what I have now,
there was nowhere left to go
but where I am,
Here and Now,
with God.

I am finding out
that every moment is unique
and therefore precious.
The sunsets I see
will never be duplicated.
The hug of a friend,
the laughter of my Granddaughters
will never be precisely repeated
or felt again.

This moment I am experiencing
can never be recaptured.

To be Present
is the only way
I can appreciate life to its fullest
and
be touched by the Wonder
of each moment.

## Judgment

I have carried in me
the voice of judgment
for so very long.
It has been directed
inward and outward,
comparing, discriminating, censuring.
Often I simply judged
on the same basis
as I had been judged.
At times,
I have been harsh, tough, cruel,
and punitive
in judging others
and myself.

Many times,
my judging was a prideful refuge
for me.
I used it to bolster
my sense of superiority
by dwelling on
the weaknesses of others.
My judgments
were the visible expression
of my disconnection
and separation from others
and from my own heart.

My judging
was the breeding ground for
my pride, pain, alienation, division.

Jesus asked me,
"Who among us has not sinned?"
I needed to cast out
the beam in my own eye,
before pointing out
the mote in others.

My judgments
found their way
into my actions.
When I judged one "unworthy"
I turned away from them.
When "attractive"
I pursued them.
Often, I simply dismissed people.

Judgments
created in me
an inner environment
lacking in Kindness and Love.

Oh, I rationalized my judgments,
convincing myself
I knew right from wrong.

Without judgment
I thought I could not make decisions.
Would not the absence of judgment
deprive me of value and ethics?

As I learned to restrain myself
from judging,
I called upon inner depths
of clarity and understanding
to discern the Truth of each moment.
As I am better able
to set aside judgments,
often left over from the past,
I connect with each
Present Moment
Fully and Freshly.

As I set aside the superficiality
of so many of my judgments,
I am able to see each moment
with great Depth and Understanding.

Setting aside judgments,
I have discovered
Humility, Forgiveness, Tolerance.

The energy I consumed
in judging
was enormous.

Re-channeling that energy,
I can better see
that the person in front of me,
who I formerly judged
is simply myself
(and Christ)
in another form,
yearning for
the same Love, Acceptance,
Openheartedness
as I.

I am learning a Great Truth:
*No matter what happens,*
*Never put anyone out of my heart,*
*No matter what happens.*

Often,
I have acted in pain, confusion, fear
creating even more
pain, confusion, fear.
My role, I now believe,
is instead to bring the Spirit
of Love, Peace, Understanding
to life.

# Faith

It is only by Faith
that I find the Courage
to make this Quest,
to travel from the known
to the unknown,
to leave conventional wisdom
with all my memorized answers
to life's challenges.

Faith
enabled me to leave behind
my sanctuaries of security
to reach for the horizons
that may be possible for me.
Faith is needed
to reach for that which is
greater than me,
God residing in me.

It is Faith
that lets me know
that in that multiplicity out there,
exists a Oneness.

When all else failed me,
I relied on Faith.

My Faith,
although inspired by
books, teachers, people, deeds,
is really within me.
It is not
a set of dogmas or beliefs,
cast in concrete,
but simply
an ability to be
comfortable in uncertainty.
Through Faith,
I can see what is True,
which strengthens my capacity
to Open.

Faith
lay dormant in me for such a long time.
I was preoccupied
with the rational, analytical, mental.
Often, I relied more on
accomplishments, achievements,
credentials
than on Intuition and trust.

On retirement,
my inner Quest
and the Holy Spirit
through Intuition
called me out of my comfort zone
and inflamed my thirst
for new horizons.
I was called
to search within myself
for the potential
I now know is possible.

Faith
has been double-edged.
Sometimes, I felt as if
I were becoming
a custodian of Truth.
But, just as soon as I put God in a box,
just as soon as I thought I knew
answers to the questions of life,
I was surprised
to learn I knew nothing.
Faith opened me
to learn from mystery
to expect and enjoy surprise.

Insecurity and self-doubt
had been my constant companions.
They tempted me to seek boundaries
rather than Horizons.

I feared aloneness.
I sought
assurance, sanction, affirmation.
Faith told me
they are not needed.

Faith
opens me,
rather than narrowing me.
Faith says
Explore, Inquire, Investigate!
Faith says
Trust the answers I discover
within me.
Faith says
Listen to the Wisdom outside,
but do not be distracted from
my Deep Inner Trust in God
resident within me.

The Great Faith
I have been discovering within me
enables me to live Fully
as a Compassionate Human Being.

**My Faith**
does not wear a frown.
It brings Humor and Great Delight.
It is so Loving and Aware
that it encompasses all
the pain, absurdities, ironies, and
complexities of my life
with a chuckle.

# Mystery

In my Quest
to Live and Love Deeply and Fully,
I am beginning to learn
to see again
with the eyes of a child,
to see each moment,
each experience,
each event,
Anew.
Eyes of innocence
are being reopened
by Sensitivity and
Loving Attention to each new moment.

Each moment Anew
acquaints me with a Universe
of Enchantment and Mystery.
The moments I can see with Freshness
without filters of judgment,
without labels,
bring Profound Stillness
and Receptivity.

In the Grace of Stillness,
I discover God within
and
Spontaneity, Creativity, Wisdom.

I worshipped
at the altar of the thinking mind.
Much of my journey
was devoted to acquisition
of knowledge, information,
and things.
Seeing the world
—and myself—
through the filter of
the information and knowledge
I had gathered
imprisoned me
with the ideas and images
I pursued.

I thought I know myself;
All I really knew,
was what I thought about myself.

When I thought I knew
the world around me,
I was barred from seeing
the mystery
held within each moment.

I learned that
my Quest does not dismiss
my Creative Power of Inquiry.
It awakens it.

My Spiritual Journey
gave me a way of seeing,
not bound by the limitations
of second-hand information.

Scriptures and Religion,
at best,
point to the presence of
the Great Mystery
before me,
within me.

I needed to unload
all my burdens of "should"
from myself
and from all those I had burdened.

As I was able to set aside
all the images I formed
from information.
I was able to connect
with each moment
in Innocence and Freshness.

I paint
the landscape of my life
with the colors of my thoughts,
values, actions, feelings.

The Quality of my life
is flavored by
the Quality of my feelings.
I make ripples
through the Universe
by my very presence.

I am really not different
than anyone else.
Not one thought, delight, feeling,
mistake I have experienced
has not been experienced
by an other.
I see myself in others
and they in me.

I am not called upon to judge,
but simply to respond with
Understanding, Kindness and Love.

What truly matters
is how I respond.
*How I hold others in my Heart
is what I will become.*

As I participate
in the creation of each moment,
I find a power
to Heal, Love, Care,
to be Compassionate.

I now know
the path is without end.

I cannot measure the worth
of a single Loving Action,
the impact of a single Caring Gesture
the results of a single Meditation.
But,
When I do them in Love,
results fade in importance.

Knowing that my deeds matter,
knowing that at my hands,
God's Healing Transformation
can take place,
has changed my life.

## Balance

I seek Balance.
I seek neither withdrawal from life,
nor over indulgence.
I seek Truth
with all my being.

The deepest joy I found
came from within me,
only when
I'd found a balanced heart.
I can't stop the waves,
but I can learn to sail them.
I can't change circumstances in my life,
but I can balance amid them
and
bring balance to them.

I am trying to learn
when Energy and Resolution
are needed
and when it is time to be Soft
and Surrender.
I am trying to learn
when Inquiry is required
and when it is time to have Faith.

I am trying to learn
when Service is needed
and when Silence and Solitude
are best.
I am trying to learn
when active Care is needed
and when it is time for Simplicity.

I am learning
that Serenity is not some lofty peak,
but simply responding with Love
to every moment's challenge.
I am learning
that Wisdom is not an attainment,
but a way of Being,
a way of Responding.

I see
endless conflict and destruction
around me.
Planet Earth suffers
as relationships break down
and individuals live in alienation.
I don't think more ideas are needed
to change things,
rather a change of Heart is required.

I try not to respond to the pain
with righteousness, formulas, or
withdrawal.
Rather I try to respond
with Integrity and Love.

# Wisdom

A big challenge I face
is making my life an embodiment of
Wisdom, Compassion, and Love.
The Truths I have discovered
need to find visible expression
in my life.
Every one of my thoughts, words,
and actions
holds the possibility of being
a visible expression of Love.

I know it's simply not enough
to be a possessor of some Wisdom.
Believing myself to be
a custodian of some truth
I became
stale,
self-righteous,
rigid.

I have not been able to live
in enlightened retirement
on the bounty of
my past achievements.

Wisdom
is only alive
when lived.
Understanding is liberating
only when it is applied.
My portfolio of spiritual experiences
is useless
unless it sustains me
through loss, change, growth.

My knowledge and my achievements
matter little
unless I touch the Heart of an other
and am touched by an other.

I live in undeniable Connectedness.
My every word,
my every action creates a ripple
in the universal pond.
My Awareness
brings Sacredness
to each moment.

Nothing
is inconsequential.
Nothing insignificant.
Spirituality
touches every aspect of my life.

My sexuality
respects and honors
all living beings.
Every relationship
offers me the chance
to Grow and Receive.
My Spirituality
will be Visible and Vital
when it embraces every facet
of my life.

## Creation

There are moments
when I stand in awe of Creation.
Every ending
is a new beginning;
Every death,
a new birth.
Awakening to the beauty of Creation
has brought me
a Peace with all things.

As I deepen in Silence,
I discover I am listening to
the rhythms of the seasons
and the expansion and contraction
of all things.
I am discovering that
all things, inner and outer,
are connected.

My youth has vanished.
It has joined history and antiquity.
Each day, each moment, appears
and then strides offstage.
When I am silent,
I can sense Creation renewing itself
moment by moment.

These moments seem bound together
by  Silence.

I begin to see
that death is not the opposite of life,
simply the a witness to birth,
both a normal part of life.
Endings signal Beginnings.
Emptiness reveals Fullness.
I strive to understand
the embrace of emptiness and fullness
in my life.
God, as nature,
abhors a vacuum,
and rushes in to fill it.

Emptiness
no longer holds fear.
Emptiness is Beautiful and Joyful.
Resting in that place
where God lives within me,
I live in Harmony
with the Universe.
Silence brings me
Wholeness, Peace, Well-Being.

I have found no standard map
to enlightenment.

It is not enough to emulate those
who have gone before.
I must learn to see with my own eyes
and to travel my own path
myself.

I can learn some fundamentals
from others,
but I must discover myself
how to bring these to Blossom.

A map is not the journey.

When I die,
God will not ask me
if I have been like John the Baptist,
John of the Cross, or
John the Evangelist.
God will ask me
if I have been truly John Chuchman.
I must let my life be a deep expression
of my heartfelt values.

## Letting Go

I am seeking depths
of Joy, Clarity, and Harmony.
I think I am on the right path
as my experiences empower me
to Transform and Liberate myself.

In being Liberated,
I discover tremendous Gratitude.
God has Cared for me
in so many beautiful ways.
I have been supported, guided,
Loved.
I long to give back to the earth
that has supported me.
Giving back
enables me to fill
the rest of my time here
with as much Compassion and Love
as possible.

My Quest
seems successful
as I am able to Let Go.

In Letting Go,
I discovered a Profound Revelation:
When I stop being full of opinions
and expectations,
I become truly Receptive.
When I stopped being afraid of loss,
I began to open up
to the world around me.
In facing aloneness,
I discovered Togetherness.
Letting Go
expresses Compassion
for myself and
the world I in which I live.

I need to let go of the past;
It's past.
I need to let go of
concern for the future;
It's in God's hands.
I need to let go of the present;
each moment passes on.
I need to let go of
expectations, fears, guilt.
Letting Go is the path to
Awakening.
Letting Go
allows me to be Fully Present.

Often, I sought spiritual compromise.
There is none.
Awakening is not negotiable.
I can't hold onto things I like
and let go of others.
A lukewarm yearning for Awakening
did not sustain me.
Besides,
anything I lost
was never truly mine.
Anything to which I clung
simply imprisoned me.

My Challenge
is to learn the Joy
of Letting Go.
Letting Go allows me
to live wisely

Letting Go of my fears and habits
allows a gracious Wisdom
to emerge.
Letting Go of beliefs and attachments
is to make the Quest
with an Open Heart.

When I can release the old,
I let the New be born in me.

I am beginning to see
I am not the owner or possessor
of things or people in my life.
I am only with them for a time.
I can live with them
Tolerantly and Wisely
or graspingly and unwisely.
Even this body
is not mine to keep.
It is a gift
to be returned
to Mother Earth.


Learning to be Truly Present,
I am discovering
that which I seek,
the object of my Quest,
God,
has always been with me
within me.

Shared in the hope
that My Quest
helps you on yours,

in Love,

John Chuchman